The Picnic

Rachel Menzies

Illustrated by Miriam Latimer

Schofield & Sims

Tig and Og pa<u>ck</u> a picnic.

Pop a mu<u>ff</u>in in the ru<u>ck</u>sa<u>ck</u>.

Tig and Og go up the hill.

Pop a rug on the mud.

Tig and Og unpa<u>ck</u> the picnic.

No, Baff! Not the picnic!

Can Tig and Og get the picnic?